UTAH

BUCKET LIST

(FULL COLOR)

Your Ultimate Guide to Breathtaking
Parks, Scenic Drives, Hidden Gems and
Unforgettable Adventures

By

DAVID E. ALVIS

TABLE OF CONTENT

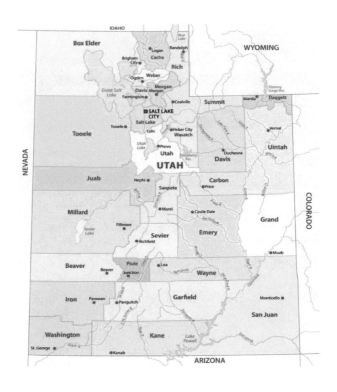

INTRODUCTION

Overview of Utah's Unique Landscape and Attractions

Utah is a state full of incredible contrasts, where red rock formations rise high above the ground and alpine forests stretch across the mountains. Its landscapes also include wide desert areas that feel endless. From the famous sandstone arches in Arches National Park to the deep and dramatic canyons in Zion National Park, Utah has a remarkable variety of natural beauty. The state is home to five famous national parks, known as the "Mighty Five," along with many state parks, making it one of the most picturesque places in the United States. Unique natural features like hoodoos, natural bridges, and narrow slot canyons make Utah a favorite destination for nature lovers, adventure seekers, and photographers.

But Utah isn't just about its natural beauty—it also has a fascinating history and culture. Visitors can see ancient rock carvings, explore the ruins of the Ancestral Puebloan people, and learn about the heritage of Salt Lake City, which is the center of the Mormon faith. With its mix of outdoor adventures, cultural sites, and delicious food, Utah has something to offer everyone.

Why Utah Belongs on Your Bucket List

Utah isn't just a place to visit, it's an experience that stays with you long after you leave. Whether you're hiking through the towering walls of the Narrows in Zion National Park, gazing at the endless stars lighting up the night sky in Canyonlands, or skiing on Park City's famous powder snow, Utah offers moments that feel magical.

The state is easy to visit and offers so much variety that it's perfect for any traveler. Whether you're looking for heart-pounding adventures or peaceful, beautiful places to relax, Utah has everything you need to create the perfect trip. The state also cares deeply about preserving its natural environment, with efforts like Leave No Trace practices and sustainable tourism, ensuring its beauty lasts for future generations.

Adding Utah to your bucket list means choosing to explore, discover, and connect with some of the most unique and extraordinary places in the world. Once you visit, the memories of Utah's wonders will stay with you forever.

PLANNING YOUR TRIP

Major Airports and Entry Points

Utah is easy to access, with several options for travelers arriving by air or road. The Salt Lake City International Airport (SLC) serves as the state's main gateway, offering numerous domestic and international flights. For those heading to southern Utah's national parks, regional airports such as St. George Regional Airport (SGU) and Cedar City Regional Airport (CDC) provide closer access. If you're driving, Utah is well-connected by major highways like Interstate 15, which runs north to south through the state, and Interstate 70, which cuts through the eastern side and provides direct access to scenic areas like Moab and Canyonlands.

Renting a Car and Navigating Scenic Routes

To truly experience Utah's beauty, renting a car is a must. Utah's attractions are spread out, and public transportation options are limited outside of cities. Most visitors pick up rental cars at Salt Lake City International Airport or other major hubs. Whether you're cruising along Highway 12, which is often called "America's Most Beautiful Drive," or exploring Monument Valley's iconic landscapes, having your own vehicle gives you the freedom to stop and soak in the views.

Utah's roadways are designed for scenic exploration, with well-maintained routes leading to almost every major attraction. If you're planning to visit remote areas, such as slot canyons or rugged trails, consider renting an SUV or a vehicle with four-wheel drive for better navigation on unpaved roads. Familiarize yourself with Utah's driving laws and be mindful of the speed limits, especially in smaller towns and near parks.

Road Trip Essentials: Safety, Gas Stations, and Rest Areas

A successful road trip in Utah requires some preparation, as services can be limited in rural and remote areas. Always keep your gas tank full when traveling to national parks or remote locations, as gas stations may be far apart. Rest areas are available along interstates and some highways, but they're less common on scenic byways, so plan your stops carefully.

Carry a road trip kit that includes water, snacks, maps, a flashlight, and basic tools. For desert areas, prepare for high temperatures during the day and cooler nights. In mountainous regions, watch for sudden weather changes, including snow or rain, which can impact driving conditions. Always check local weather forecasts before heading out, as flash floods can occur in desert canyons during rainy seasons.

Travelers in Utah often find that the journey is just as memorable as the destination. With a bit of planning and the right gear, exploring Utah by road will be a safe and unforgettable experience.

ACCOMMODATION OPTIONS

Utah has a variety of places to stay, catering to every kind of traveler. From luxurious resorts with world-class amenities to cozy hotels offering a relaxing escape, there's something for everyone. Whether you're exploring Utah's natural wonders or enjoying the city's attractions, the state's accommodations ensure a comfortable and unforgettable experience.

Best Hotels and Resorts for Comfort

Utah's top hotels and resorts offer excellent service, comfortable rooms, and great locations, making them perfect for a relaxing and enjoyable stay.

- **Grand America Hotel (Salt Lake City)**

This five-star luxury hotel in downtown Salt Lake City features spacious rooms, elegant décor, and high-end amenities. Guests can unwind at the full-service spa, swim in the outdoor pool, and enjoy fine dining. Its central location makes it an ideal base for visiting Temple Square and nearby attractions.

- **Amangiri (Canyon Point)**

Situated in southern Utah's stunning red rock desert, Amangiri is a luxury resort renowned for its minimalist design and peaceful surroundings. It offers private suites, a tranquil spa, and an infinity pool with incredible desert views. It's perfect for those looking for a secluded, serene getaway.

- **Stein Eriksen Lodge (Park City)**

This award-winning ski-in/ski-out resort in Deer Valley blends alpine charm with modern luxury. Spacious suites, a world-class spa, and gourmet dining make it an excellent choice for both winter sports enthusiasts and summer adventurers.

- **Cliffrose Springdale (Near Zion National Park)**

Located just outside the entrance to Zion National Park, this boutique hotel combines comfort and convenience. It features cozy rooms, breathtaking views of the cliffs, and easy access to hiking trails. Guests can relax by the riverside pool and enjoy the beautifully landscaped gardens.

- **Sorrel River Ranch Resort (Moab)**

This upscale resort, located along the Colorado River, offers rustic luxury with stunning views of red rock formations. Guests can enjoy horseback riding, yoga, guided hikes, and other activities, making it a great destination for relaxation and adventure.

- **The St. Regis Deer Valley (Park City)**

Known for its outstanding service and luxurious rooms, this mountain resort features a world-class spa and fine dining options. With ski-in/ski-out access in winter and trails for hiking and biking in summer, it's a top choice year-round.

- **Zermatt Resort (Midway)**

Inspired by a Swiss alpine village, Zermatt Resort offers European-style charm with spacious rooms, a spa, and on-site dining. It's a great option for both romantic getaways and family vacations, set in a scenic mountain location.

- **Desert Pearl Inn (Springdale)**

Located near Zion National Park, this boutique inn offers stylish, spacious accommodations with views of the Virgin River and canyon walls. Its peaceful setting and outdoor pool make it a favorite for those exploring Zion.

- **Lodge at Bryce Canyon (Bryce Canyon National Park)**

Nestled within Bryce Canyon National Park, this historic lodge offers rustic cabins and comfortable rooms surrounded by the park's famous hoodoos. Staying here allows visitors to experience the park's beauty at sunrise and sunset without needing a long drive.

Whether you're looking for a luxurious retreat in the mountains, a peaceful escape in the desert, or convenient lodging near Utah's iconic parks, the state's accommodations provide comfort and quality for every kind of traveler.

Budget-Friendly Camping and RV Parks

Utah is a paradise for outdoor lovers, offering plenty of affordable camping and RV options. Whether you're looking for a peaceful spot in the mountains, a campsite near a national park, or a well-equipped RV park with modern amenities, Utah has everything you need. Here's a closer look at some great choices for budget-friendly accommodations:

National Park and State Park Campgrounds

Zion National Park Campgrounds:

- **Watchman Campground:** Just a short walk from the park's visitor center, this campground offers affordable sites with breathtaking views of Zion's towering cliffs. Amenities include flush toilets, drinkable water, and RV hookups.

- **South Campground:** Another budget-friendly option, this campground is ideal for tent campers. It's close to the park's shuttle system and provides basic facilities like restrooms, picnic tables, and drinking water.

Bryce Canyon National Park Campgrounds:

- **North Campground**: Situated near the famous Bryce Amphitheater, this campground is perfect for those exploring the park's hoodoos. It accommodates both tents and RVs and includes essentials like potable water and restrooms.

- **Sunset Campground**: Located near Sunset Point, this quieter option offers similar amenities and provides easy access to some of Bryce Canyon's most scenic trails.

Dead Horse Point State Park Campground:

Known for its stunning views of the Colorado River, this campground is ideal for stargazing and hiking enthusiasts. It offers budget-friendly tent sites and RV spaces, some with hookups, and gives visitors a chance to immerse themselves in the park's incredible desert landscapes.

BLM (Bureau of Land Management) and Dispersed Camping

For those seeking a more adventurous and cost-effective stay, Utah's BLM-managed lands offer free or low-cost dispersed camping in some of the state's most scenic areas.

- **Moab BLM Camping**
  Moab has several first-come, first-served BLM campgrounds, including Goose Island and Hittle Bottom, both located along the Colorado River. These sites are affordable

and close to Arches and Canyonlands National Parks, making them convenient for adventurers.

Grand Staircase-Escalante National Monument:

Dispersed camping is allowed in many parts of this monument, offering a budget-friendly way to experience Utah's rugged backcountry. These remote sites require campers to bring their own water and supplies for a self-sufficient stay.

Private RV Parks

If you're traveling by RV and prefer more amenities, private parks are an excellent option. They combine affordability with added conveniences.

- **Zion River Resort (Virgin):** This RV park offers full hookups, laundry services, and a swimming pool, all at reasonable rates. Its location near Zion National Park makes it a top pick for RV travelers.

- **Moab Valley RV Resort & Campground**: Perfect for families, this campground offers a mix of RV sites, tent spaces, and cabins. Guests can enjoy a pool, hot tub, and playground, making it a comfortable and family-friendly choice.

Unique Stays: Yurts, Cabins, and Glamping

For those looking for a unique and memorable experience, Utah offers a variety of special accommodations. From rustic yurts to luxury glamping tents, these options let you connect with nature while enjoying a comfortable stay.

Yurt Stays

- **East Canyon State Park Yurts (Morgan)**

These cozy, affordable yurts come equipped with bunk beds, heaters, and picnic tables. Located in a scenic mountain area, they're great for families and groups seeking a peaceful escape.

- **Dead Horse Point State Park Yurts (Moab)**

Perched above the canyons of the Colorado River, these yurts offer stunning views and a tranquil setting. Each yurt includes a bed, futon, and an outdoor deck, making it a unique retreat for stargazers and adventurers.

- **Wasatch Mountain State Park Yurts (Midway)**

Perfect for year-round stays, these yurts provide easy access to hiking trails in the summer and skiing in the winter. They feature heating, lighting, and nearby restrooms for added convenience.

Cabins

- **Capitol Reef Resort (Torrey)**

These charming cabins blend rustic design with modern amenities. Guests can enjoy incredible views of Capitol Reef's red rock cliffs while staying close to hiking and other outdoor activities.

- **Bear Lake State Park Cabins (Garden City)**
Located by the serene waters of Bear Lake, these cabins are equipped with kitchens, cozy living areas, and outdoor patios. Visitors can swim, fish, or kayak just steps from their door.

- **Flaming Gorge Resort Cabins (Dutch John)**
Ideal for fishing and boating enthusiasts, these cabins near Flaming Gorge Reservoir are fully furnished and provide a comfortable retreat after a day of outdoor adventures.

Glamping

- **Under Canvas Moab**
Located near Arches and Canyonlands National Parks, this glamping site features safari-style tents with luxurious touches like plush beds, private bathrooms, and wood-burning stoves. Guests can also participate in guided hikes and yoga classes.

- **Zion Wildflower Resort (Virgin)**

Offering a mix of glamping tents, covered wagons, and tiny homes, this resort provides stunning views of Zion National Park. Guests can relax around fire pits and enjoy the communal atmosphere.

- **Conestoga Ranch (Bear Lake)**

This upscale glamping resort features covered wagons and luxury tents with high-end amenities. Located near Bear Lake, it's perfect for enjoying outdoor activities and breathtaking views while staying in comfort.

Utah's camping and unique accommodations offer something for every traveler. Whether you're pitching a tent, parking your RV, staying in a yurt, or glamping in style, these options let you experience Utah's stunning landscapes while creating unforgettable memories.

LOCAL CUISINE AND UNIQUE DINING

Utah's food scene is as diverse as its landscapes, offering a mix of traditional Western comfort food and innovative modern dishes. From classic regional specialties to creative culinary experiences, Utah has something for every kind of food lover. Whether you're enjoying a hearty meal at a cozy diner, savoring fresh produce at a farm-to-table restaurant, or indulging in sweet treats at a roadside stop, the state's food culture will leave a lasting impression.

Must-Try Dishes and Regional Flavors

Utah's food reflects its pioneer roots and local ingredients, with a unique twist on classic recipes. Here are some must-try dishes and regional favorites:

•**Fry Sauce**

Fry sauce is a Utah original, made by mixing ketchup and mayonnaise, often with added spices or pickle juice. This tangy and creamy condiment is served with fries, burgers, onion rings, and more, and is a staple across the state's eateries.

•Funeral Potatoes

A comfort food favorite, funeral potatoes are a cheesy casserole made with shredded or cubed potatoes, sour cream, cheese, and a crunchy topping like cornflakes or breadcrumbs. While often served at gatherings, they've become a beloved dish at restaurants and potlucks alike.

•Utah Scones

Utah's version of scones is more like fry bread. These deep-fried doughy treats are served warm and topped with honey, powdered sugar, or jam. They're popular at breakfast spots, fairs, and local diners.

•Pastry Cream Pie and Pie Shakes

Utah takes desserts to the next level with pie shakes, milkshakes blended with slices of pie. Rich cream pies, such as banana or chocolate, are a local specialty and a perfect indulgence for dessert lovers.

•Bear Lake Raspberries

These sweet and flavorful raspberries, grown near Bear Lake, are often used in shakes, pies, and jams. A Bear Lake Raspberry Shake is a must-try when visiting the area.

•Dutch Oven Cooking

Dating back to pioneer times, Dutch oven cooking remains a beloved tradition in Utah. Cast-iron pots are used to prepare slow-cooked stews, baked beans, and desserts like fruit cobblers over an open fire.

•Freshwater Trout

With Utah's abundance of lakes and rivers, trout is a popular menu item. Whether grilled, smoked, or pan-fried, locally caught trout is a highlight of many meals.

•Jell-O

Utah's unique love for Jell-O, particularly lime-flavored, has earned it the title of "Jell-O Capital of the World." This nostalgic treat is often served with fruit or whipped cream at family and community events.

Memorable Restaurants and Food Stops Across Utah

Utah's dining scene offers a variety of options, from casual cafés to elegant restaurants. Each region showcases unique flavors and warm hospitality.

Salt Lake City:

- **The Roof Restaurant:** Located in the Joseph Smith Memorial Building, this upscale restaurant offers panoramic views of Temple Square. The menu features gourmet dishes and decadent desserts, making it perfect for a special evening.

- **Red Iguana:** Famous for its authentic Mexican cuisine, Red Iguana is best known for its flavorful mole sauces, which are served in several rich and unique varieties.

- **Eva's Bakery:** This French-inspired café serves artisan bread, pastries, and delicious meals in a charming, cozy atmosphere.

Park City:

- **Grub Steak Restaurant**: A Western-style steakhouse known for its premium cuts of beef, fresh seafood, and extensive wine list. The rustic décor adds to the dining experience.

- **Riverhorse on Main**: Recognized as one of Utah's top restaurants, Riverhorse offers creative dishes like macadamia nut-crusted halibut and wild game meatloaf in an elegant setting.

Southern Utah:

- **Hell's Backbone Grill & Farm (Boulder):** An award-winning farm-to-table restaurant that highlights sustainability, offering dishes made with fresh, local ingredients like lamb, trout, and seasonal vegetables.

- **Oscar's Café (Springdale):** Located near Zion National Park, this casual spot serves hearty portions of Southwestern favorites, including burgers, tacos, and enchiladas.

Small-Town Gems:

- **Capitol Reef Inn & Café (Torrey):** This quaint café offers home-style meals, including hearty breakfasts and delicious pies. It's a welcoming spot to recharge after exploring Capitol Reef National Park.

- **The Branding Iron Steakhouse (Cedar City):** A local favorite for classic American dishes like steaks, BBQ, and burgers, served in a rustic yet cozy setting.

- **Bear Lake Raspberry Shakes (Multiple Locations):** Numerous diners and stands around Bear Lake serve these famous shakes made with fresh raspberries and creamy ice cream.

Unique Dining Experiences:

- **Slackwater Pub & Pizzeria (Ogden and Sandy):** Known for its creative pizzas and wide selection of craft beers, Slackwater is a favorite among locals and visitors. Try their unique toppings like smoked trout or jalapeños.

- **Log Haven (Salt Lake City):** Set in a historic log cabin in Millcreek Canyon, Log

Haven offers a romantic dining experience with upscale dishes like bison short ribs and wild mushroom tart.

Utah's culinary landscape is a blend of tradition and creativity. Whether you're savoring local classics like fry sauce or enjoying a fine-dining experience with fresh, locally sourced ingredients, every meal in Utah tells a story of its rich culture and flavors. From small-town eateries to gourmet restaurants, Utah's food scene is as memorable as its stunning scenery.

SAMPLE ITINERARIES

Weekend Getaway: Highlights of Utah in 3 Days

Even with just a few days, Utah offers plenty of amazing experiences. Here's a suggested plan for a memorable 3-day trip:

Day 1: Salt Lake City to Arches National Park

Begin your adventure in Salt Lake City, Utah's lively capital. Start the day with a visit to Temple Square, a peaceful and historic site, then grab a hearty breakfast at a local café. After exploring the city, drive to Moab, a town known for its outdoor activities and proximity to two national parks. Spend the afternoon at Arches National Park, where you can hike to Delicate Arch, one of Utah's most iconic landmarks, and explore the Windows Section, home to impressive rock formations. End the day in downtown Moab, where you'll find great dining and a fun atmosphere.

Day 2: Canyonlands National Park and Dead Horse Point

On your second day, visit Canyonlands National Park, starting on the Island in the Sky district. Be sure to take the short hike to Mesa Arch early in the morning to see the sunrise through the arch, a perfect photo spot. Stop by Grand View Point for incredible views of the canyons below. In the afternoon, head to Dead Horse Point State Park, just outside Canyonlands, for stunning overlooks of the Colorado River. Pack a picnic to enjoy while taking in the breathtaking scenery. Return to Moab for the night.

Day 3: Zion National Park

On your last day, drive south to Zion National Park, one of Utah's most famous destinations. Take a scenic drive through Zion Canyon, stopping for short walks like the Riverside Walk or Weeping Rock. If you're up for a challenge, hike Angels Landing, a thrilling trail with jaw-dropping views. Spend the afternoon exploring Zion's beauty before heading back to Salt Lake City or your next stop.

One-Week Adventure: The Mighty 5 National Parks

A week in Utah is the perfect amount of time to explore all five of its famous national parks.

Day 1-2: Zion National Park

Start at Zion National Park, Utah's most visited park. Spend the first day exploring Zion Canyon, taking the shuttle to stops like Court of the Patriarchs and The Grotto. Hike the Emerald Pools Trail for views of waterfalls and lush scenery. On the second day, try the more adventurous The Narrows, where you hike through a river surrounded by towering canyon walls, or tackle the challenging Angels Landing for breathtaking views. Stay both nights in Springdale, a nearby town with great accommodations and restaurants.

Day 3: Bryce Canyon National Park

Drive about two hours to Bryce Canyon National Park, known for its unique hoodoos, tall, thin rock spires. Begin with a sunrise at Sunrise Point, then hike the Navajo Loop and Queen's Garden trails to get up close to these formations. Visit overlooks like Bryce Point and Inspiration Point for panoramic views of the canyon. Stay overnight in the small towns of Tropic or Panguitch.

Day 4-5: Capitol Reef National Park

From Bryce, take the scenic Highway 12, a road known for its incredible views, to Capitol Reef

National Park. Spend the first day exploring the Fruita Historic District, where you can see orchards and historic buildings. Take a short hike to Hickman Bridge, a beautiful natural arch. On the second day, drive through Capitol Gorge to see ancient petroglyphs and unique rock formations. For adventurous travelers, hike to Cassidy Arch or visit the Waterpocket Fold, a massive geological feature. Stay in Torrey, a small town near the park.

Day 6: Arches National Park

Next, drive to Moab, your base for visiting Arches National Park. Spend the day exploring the park's famous rock formations, including Delicate Arch, Landscape Arch, and Double Arch. The Windows Section is also a must-see for multiple arches in one area. After a day of exploring, enjoy dinner at a local Moab restaurant and rest for your final adventure.

Day 7: Canyonlands National Park

Wrap up your trip with a visit to Canyonlands National Park, focusing on the Island in the Sky district. Start the day with sunrise at Mesa Arch, then head to Grand View Point for stunning views of the vast canyon landscapes. If you have extra time, explore the quieter Needles district, known for its colorful spires and hiking trails. On your way back, stop at Dead Horse Point State Park for one last breathtaking view of the Colorado River before concluding your Utah adventure.

This week-long plan ensures you experience Utah's best sights, from its famous parks to its hidden gems, leaving you with unforgettable memories.

Off-the-Beaten-Path: Hidden Gems in 7 Days

If you want to avoid crowds and explore Utah's hidden treasures, this 7-day itinerary will guide you to some of the most beautiful and lesser-known spots in the state.

Day 1: Goblin Valley State Park and Little Wild Horse Canyon

Begin your trip at Goblin Valley State Park, a place filled with strange, mushroom-shaped rock formations that look like they belong on another planet. Spend the morning walking among these fascinating "goblins" and taking in the unusual scenery. In the afternoon, visit Little Wild Horse Canyon, a nearby slot canyon that offers a fun and moderately easy hike through narrow, winding rock passages. It's a great spot for families and perfect for taking photos. Stay overnight in Green River, a small town with convenient places to stay.

Day 2: Nine Mile Canyon

Drive to Nine Mile Canyon, often called the "world's longest art gallery." This remote area is full of ancient petroglyphs and pictographs made by the Fremont and Ute people. Take your time exploring the detailed rock art and learning about the history of the region. Be sure to bring plenty of water and snacks since there aren't many services nearby. Spend the night in Price, a nearby town with comfortable accommodations and dining options.

Day 3: Capitol Reef National Park's Cathedral Valley

Visit the less-visited Cathedral Valley area of Capitol Reef National Park, known for its impressive sandstone monoliths like the Temple of the Sun and Temple of the Moon. You'll need a high-clearance or 4WD vehicle to reach this remote area, but the stunning views are worth the effort. Don't miss Glass Mountain, a mound of sparkling gypsum crystals that's truly unique. Stay overnight in Torrey, a small town close to the park.

Day 4: Fishlake National Forest and Pando Grove

Head to Fishlake National Forest, home to Pando, the world's largest living organism. This massive grove of quaking aspens is all connected by a single root system and covers more than 100 acres. Enjoy a quiet hike or a relaxing picnic by Fish Lake, a beautiful alpine lake surrounded by lush greenery. At night, look up and enjoy the stars before staying in a cozy cabin or lodge near the forest.

Day 5: Dead Horse Point State Park

Travel to Dead Horse Point State Park, a hidden gem near Canyonlands National Park. The park offers jaw-dropping views of the Colorado River winding through the desert and dramatic cliffs. Take the East Rim Trail for quieter, less crowded views, and enjoy a picnic at one of the park's scenic spots. Afterward, head to Moab for the night, where you'll find plenty of restaurants and lodging options.

Day 6: Cedar Breaks National Monument

Explore Cedar Breaks National Monument, a lesser-known spot often compared to a smaller version of Bryce Canyon. The park features colorful rock formations, alpine meadows, and, in the summer, bright wildflowers. Take the Spectra Point Trail for incredible views of the canyon and surrounding mountains. Spend the night in Brian Head, a nearby resort town with warm and comfortable lodging options.

Day 7: Coral Pink Sand Dunes State Park

End your trip at Coral Pink Sand Dunes State Park, where you can walk across soft, pink-colored sand dunes. This peaceful and uncrowded park is perfect for sandboarding, hiking, or off-road adventures. Take your time exploring the unique beauty of the dunes and enjoy a quiet, relaxing finish to your Utah adventure.

This 7-day itinerary highlights some of Utah's most beautiful and lesser-known spots, providing a peaceful and memorable way to explore the state's stunning landscapes.

TOP NATURAL WONDERS

Utah is a land of remarkable natural beauty, featuring an extraordinary mix of landscapes that range from towering sandstone cliffs to sprawling desert plains, lush forests, and otherworldly rock formations. These natural wonders have drawn millions of visitors, making Utah one of the most awe-inspiring destinations in the United States. Below is a detailed guide to Utah's top natural wonders, designed to give you a deep appreciation of each site and help you plan an unforgettable visit.

Arches National Park: Iconic Rock Formations

Arches National Park, located near Moab, is a geological masterpiece, home to over 2,000 natural sandstone arches that have been shaped by millions of years of wind and water erosion. Each formation is unique, creating a landscape that feels almost alien.

- **Delicate Arch:** The park's most famous feature and a symbol of Utah itself, Delicate Arch is a freestanding marvel that stands 46 feet high and 32 feet wide. The 3-mile roundtrip hike to reach it is moderately challenging, taking you across slickrock trails and gentle inclines. Seeing this arch at sunset, when the rock glows orange and red, is an experience you'll never forget.

- **Landscape Arch**: One of the world's longest natural arches, spanning 290 feet. This impossibly thin arch looks delicate, yet it has stood the test of time. Located along the Devils Garden Trail, it's a must-see for anyone visiting the park.

- **Double Arch:** Known for its towering size, Double Arch consists of two arches that share the same foundation, making it one of the park's most photographed features. The short walk to this site makes it accessible for visitors of all ages.

- **Windows Section**: This area is a treasure trove of formations, including North Window, South Window, and Turret Arch, all located close together. It's an ideal spot for photography, particularly at sunrise or sunset.

The park also boasts features like Balanced Rock, Courthouse Towers, and Fiery Furnace, each offering its own unique beauty. Whether you're a seasoned hiker or just looking for a scenic drive, Arches National Park has something for everyone.

Zion National Park: A Hiker's Paradise

Zion National Park, Utah's first national park, is a haven for adventurers and nature lovers. Its towering red cliffs, lush greenery, and dramatic canyons make it one of the most visited parks in the country.

- **Angels Landing**: This trail is both thrilling and challenging, offering a 5.4-mile roundtrip hike that culminates in panoramic views of Zion Canyon. The final stretch involves a narrow ridge with steep drop-offs, but the reward is one of the most stunning vistas in the park.

- **The Narrows:** This unique hike takes you through the Virgin River, where you'll wade through water surrounded by towering canyon walls. The hike is as refreshing as it is breathtaking, making it an unforgettable experience.

- **Emerald Pools**: A series of pools and waterfalls accessible via three different trails, Lower, Middle, and Upper Emerald Pools. This family-friendly hike showcases the park's lush vegetation and serene water features.

- **Observation Point:** For those seeking a less crowded alternative to Angels Landing, Observation Point offers equally spectacular views of the canyon. The 8-mile roundtrip hike is strenuous but well worth the effort.

- **Riverside Walk**: A paved, easy trail that leads to the entrance of The Narrows, perfect for visitors of all ages and abilities.

Zion also features the Zion-Mount Carmel Highway, a scenic drive with incredible switchbacks and tunnels carved into the rock, providing breathtaking views of the park. Wildlife such as mule deer, bighorn sheep, and a variety of birds are commonly spotted throughout the park, adding to its charm.

Bryce Canyon National Park: Hoodoo Heaven

Bryce Canyon National Park is a natural amphitheater filled with hoodoos, towering rock spires created by erosion. The park's colorful formations, ranging from orange to pink to white, create a magical, otherworldly landscape.

- **Bryce Amphitheater**: This massive natural amphitheater is the park's centerpiece, home to thousands of hoodoos. The viewpoints, including Sunrise Point, Sunset Point, Inspiration Point, and Bryce Point, offer different perspectives of the amphitheater throughout the day.

- **Navajo Loop and Queen's Garden Trails:** These trails take you into the heart of the amphitheater, allowing you to walk among the hoodoos. Highlights include Wall Street, a narrow canyon flanked by towering rock walls, and Queen Victoria, a hoodoo that resembles a statue of the British monarch.

- **Thor's Hammer:** One of the park's most iconic hoodoos, this formation resembles a hammer raised to the sky and is a favorite among photographers.

Bryce Canyon is also renowned for its night skies, earning recognition as an International Dark Sky Park. Stargazing here is an unparalleled experience, with countless stars visible on clear nights.

Canyonlands National Park: Rugged and Vast

Canyonlands National Park is a sprawling expanse of canyons, mesas, and rivers, divided into four districts: Island in the Sky, The Needles, The Maze, and the Rivers. Each district offers a unique experience.

- **Island in the Sky**: The most accessible district, featuring overlooks like Grand View Point and Green River Overlook, which provide sweeping vistas of the park's rugged terrain. Mesa Arch, a short hike from the main road, is particularly stunning at sunrise.

- **The Needles:** Known for its colorful rock spires and challenging backcountry trails, this district is perfect for hikers and campers looking for a quieter experience.

- **The Maze:** One of the most remote and challenging areas, suitable only for experienced adventurers. The Maze offers a sense of solitude and untouched wilderness.

- **The Green and Colorado Rivers:** These rivers carve through the park, creating dramatic canyons and offering opportunities for rafting and kayaking.

With its vast, untamed landscapes, Canyonlands is a paradise for explorers seeking adventure and solitude.

Monument Valley: Iconic Desert Views

Monument Valley, located on the Utah-Arizona border, is a striking desert landscape of towering sandstone buttes and mesas. It's a sacred site for the Navajo Nation and a popular filming location for Western movies.

- **Mittens and Merrick Buttes:** These iconic formations are best viewed at sunrise or sunset when the desert glows with rich, warm colors.

- **Valley Drive:** A 17-mile loop road takes you through the heart of the valley, offering close-up views of the formations. Guided tours are also available, providing deeper insight into the area's history and Navajo culture.

- **John Ford's Point:** A famous overlook that offers a perfect photo opportunity and stunning views of the valley.

These detailed descriptions of Utah's natural wonders showcase the state's diverse and awe-inspiring landscapes. Each site offers its own unique beauty, inviting visitors to explore, marvel, and create unforgettable memories.

ADVENTURE ACTIVITIES AND OUTDOOR EXPERIENCES

Utah is a dream destination for anyone who loves the outdoors. It offers a huge variety of activities for people of all skill levels, whether you prefer easy hikes, challenging climbs, or thrilling canyoneering adventures. The state's diverse landscapes make it perfect for exploration and excitement. Here's a detailed look at some of the best adventure activities you can enjoy in Utah.

Hiking Trails: From Easy Walks to Challenging Treks

Utah has an incredible network of hiking trails that range from easy, family-friendly walks to demanding trails for experienced hikers.

Easy Trails:

- **Riverside Walk (Zion National Park):** This paved trail is perfect for families or those looking for a relaxed hike. It runs along the Virgin River and leads to the start of The Narrows. The views of the canyon walls and the greenery along the trail make it a peaceful and scenic walk.

- **Dead Horse Point Rim Trail (Dead Horse Point State Park)**: This flat, easy trail follows the rim of the canyon and provides breathtaking views of the Colorado River. It's a great option for anyone looking to enjoy stunning desert landscapes without a strenuous climb.

- **Fisher Towers Trail (Near Moab):** This 4.4-mile roundtrip trail takes you through a desert landscape filled with towering rock spires. It's a moderately easy hike with incredible photo opportunities along the way.

Moderate Trails:

- **Navajo Loop and Queen's Garden Trails (Bryce Canyon National Park**): These two trails combine to form a 3-mile loop that takes you right into the heart of Bryce Canyon's iconic hoodoos. The trails are moderately challenging due to some inclines but offer unforgettable views of the unique rock formations.

- **Corona Arch Trail (Near Moab):** This 3-mile roundtrip hike leads to the stunning Corona Arch. The trail includes a bit of rock scrambling, which adds an element of adventure while still being manageable for most hikers.

Challenging Treks:

- **Angels Landing (Zion National Park):** This 5.4-mile trail is one of the most famous hikes in Utah, but it's not for the faint-hearted. It includes steep switchbacks and a narrow ridge with chains for support. At the top, you'll be rewarded with incredible views of Zion Canyon.

- **The Narrows (Zion National Park):** This hike takes you through the Virgin River, where you'll wade between towering canyon walls. You can choose a short day hike or the full 16-mile top-down route if you have a permit.

- **Delicate Arch Trail (Arches National Park):** This 3-mile roundtrip hike takes you to Utah's most famous landmark, Delicate Arch. The trail includes slickrock sections and some steep climbs, but the view of the arch is well worth the effort.

Utah's hiking trails offer something for everyone, from peaceful walks to adrenaline-pumping treks, all surrounded by breathtaking natural beauty.

Rock Climbing and Canyoneering Adventures

Utah's rugged landscapes make it a top destination for rock climbing and canyoneering. Whether you're scaling cliffs or exploring narrow slot canyons, these activities provide exciting and unforgettable experiences.

Rock Climbing:

- **Moab**: Known as Utah's rock climbing capital, Moab offers climbing options for all levels. Popular spots include Wall Street, a roadside climbing area great for beginners, and Castle Valley, home to iconic formations like Castleton Tower.

- **Little Cottonwood Canyon (Near Salt Lake City)**: This granite climbing area has routes for everyone, from beginner-friendly slabs to challenging multi-pitch climbs. It's a favorite spot for climbers near the city.

- **Maple Canyon:** Famous for its unique conglomerate rock, Maple Canyon is a paradise for climbers. It features hundreds of bolted sport routes, ranging from easy climbs to advanced challenges.

Canyoneering:

- **The Subway (Zion National Park):** This technical route is a canyoneering favorite. It involves rappelling, swimming, and navigating narrow passages through tubular canyon walls. It's a bucket-list experience for adventurous visitors.

- **Buckskin Gulch (Paria Canyon-Vermilion Cliffs Wilderness):** Known as the longest and deepest slot canyon in the world, Buckskin Gulch offers a stunning journey through towering sandstone walls. The canyon's light beams and colors are unforgettable.

- **Peek-a-Boo and Spooky Gulches (Grand Staircase-Escalante National Monument):** These slot canyons are both beautiful and challenging, requiring you to squeeze through tight spaces and climb short obstacles. They're a great choice for those looking for a unique adventure.

While rock climbing and canyoneering offer incredible experiences, they require preparation and caution. Many routes and canyons are remote, and weather conditions like flash floods can be dangerous. Beginners or those tackling technical routes are advised to hire a guide for safety.

Utah's adventure activities show off the state's natural diversity and provide endless opportunities for exploration. Whether you're hiking to stunning viewpoints, scaling rock faces, or navigating slot canyons, these experiences will create lasting memories and inspire your love for the outdoors.

Skiing and Snowboarding: Utah's Powder Paradise

Utah is famous for its top-tier skiing and snowboarding, often referred to as "The Greatest Snow on Earth." Its unique climate and geography create light, fluffy powder snow that attracts winter sports enthusiasts from all over the world. No matter your skill level, Utah's ski resorts provide slopes and facilities that cater to everyone, from beginners to seasoned pros.

- **Park City Mountain Resort**: As one of the largest ski resorts in the country, Park City offers more than 7,300 acres of terrain, with trails suited for all abilities. Its well-maintained slopes, terrain parks, and breathtaking views make it a favorite among skiers and snowboarders. The resort's reputation is further enhanced by its role as a venue during the 2002 Winter Olympics.

- **Deer Valley Resort**: Known for luxury and exclusivity, Deer Valley restricts the number of skiers on the mountain each day and doesn't allow snowboarding. This ensures uncrowded runs and a premium experience. Its immaculate slopes, excellent service, and high-end amenities make it a top choice for those seeking a more refined skiing adventure.

- **Alta Ski Area**: One of Utah's oldest resorts, Alta is a skier-only destination, famous for its deep, powdery snow and challenging terrain. It's a paradise for experienced skiers looking for some of the best powder runs in the state.

- **Snowbird**: Nestled in Little Cottonwood Canyon, Snowbird is known for its steep slopes and incredible mountain scenery. It's a favorite among advanced skiers and snowboarders who enjoy off-piste and backcountry adventures.

- **Brighton Resort**: Brighton is a family-friendly resort ideal for beginners and budget-conscious travelers. It offers affordable lift tickets, an inviting atmosphere, and excellent terrain for both skiing and snowboarding.

Utah's ski season typically lasts from November to April, with many resorts seeing significant snowfall well into spring. Beyond the slopes, visitors can enjoy après-ski activities such as gourmet dining, relaxing spa treatments, and lively entertainment. This makes Utah a perfect destination for a complete winter getaway.

Water Sports at Lake Powell

Lake Powell, a beautiful reservoir on the Colorado River, spans southern Utah and northern Arizona.

With over 2,000 miles of shoreline, surrounded by red rock cliffs and clear blue waters, it's a haven for water sports and outdoor enthusiasts.

- **Boating**: Boating is one of the best ways to explore Lake Powell's hidden coves, sandy beaches, and narrow canyons. Renting a powerboat or houseboat is a popular option, offering the freedom to navigate the lake at your own pace. Houseboats come with conveniences like kitchens, bathrooms, and sleeping areas, making them ideal for extended stays.

- **Kayaking and Paddleboarding**: The calm waters of Lake Powell are perfect for kayaking and stand-up paddleboarding. Gliding through narrow canyons like Antelope Canyon or Labyrinth Canyon gives you an up-close look at the stunning rock formations and peaceful environment.

- **Jet Skiing:** For thrill-seekers, jet skiing is an exciting way to explore the lake. The wide-open water allows for high-speed fun, while the dramatic desert scenery makes the experience unforgettable.

- **Swimming**: The lake's warm, crystal-clear water makes it a perfect place for swimming. Many secluded beaches along the shoreline provide peaceful spots to relax and take a refreshing dip.

- **Fishing**: Lake Powell is a great destination for anglers, with species such as striped bass, largemouth bass, and catfish found in its waters. You can fish from a boat or try your luck in designated fishing areas around the lake.

One of Lake Powell's most iconic attractions is Rainbow Bridge National Monument, one of the world's largest natural bridges. Accessible only by boat, it's a stunning side trip that showcases the lake's geological wonders.

Lake Powell is best visited from late spring to early fall when the weather is warm, and the water is inviting. Whether you're looking for an adventurous day on the water or a relaxing getaway surrounded by nature, Lake Powell offers something for everyone.

Best Seasonal Activities in Utah

Utah's wide variety of landscapes and its unique weather make it an amazing place to visit any time of the year. Each season offers something special, from colorful wildflowers in spring to snow-covered mountains in winter. Here's a closer look at the best activities to enjoy in every season.

Spring: Wildflower Hikes

Spring in Utah is a magical time when the state's deserts and mountains burst into life with beautiful wildflowers. The mild weather and vibrant scenery make it a perfect season for hiking.

- **Albion Basin (Little Cottonwood Canyon):** This area is famous for its wildflower displays, which bloom in late spring and early summer. Flowers like Indian paintbrush, columbines, and lupines create a colorful carpet. The Cecret Lake Trail is a great hike for families, offering stunning views of the flowers surrounded by rugged mountain peaks.

- **Capitol Reef National Park**: In spring, this park is dotted with bright wildflowers such as primrosues and penstemons. Trails like the Grand Wash Trail and Fremont River Trail are perfect for seeing these blooms while enjoying the park's desert scenery.

- **Antelope Island State Park**: This park combines wildflowers and wildlife in spring. Trails like Buffalo Point and Ladyfinger Point offer views of Great Salt Lake with wildflowers covering the paths, making it a peaceful spot for a spring hike.

Summer: Stargazing

Utah's open spaces and clear skies make it one of the best places in the world for stargazing. During the warm summer months, many of Utah's parks become perfect spots to see the stars, and several are designated as International Dark Sky Parks.

- **Bryce Canyon National Park**: Bryce is famous for its night skies, offering ranger-led astronomy programs and special stargazing events. On clear nights, you can see thousands of stars and even the Milky Way.

- **Canyonlands National Park**: This park's remote location keeps it free of light pollution, making it an ideal spot for stargazing. Grand View Point and Island in the Sky are two popular places to view the night sky.

- **Dead Horse Point State Park**: Known for its daytime views of the Colorado River, this park is equally spectacular at night. It often hosts astronomy events and is a great place to enjoy peaceful stargazing.

Fall: Fall Colors

Utah's autumn months bring breathtaking fall colors, as aspen trees, maples, and oaks turn vibrant shades of yellow, orange, and red. The cooler weather and beautiful scenery make it an excellent season for outdoor adventures.

- **Alpine Loop Scenic Byway**: This winding road near Provo offers some of the most stunning fall foliage in the state. It passes through golden aspen forests and provides views of Mount Timpanogos and Sundance Resort.

- **Zion National Park**: Zion's cottonwood trees turn a brilliant yellow in fall, adding bright colors to the park's iconic red rock landscapes. Trails like the Riverside Walk and Emerald Pools Trail are ideal for enjoying the autumn scenery.

- **Fishlake National Forest**: This forest is home to Pando, the world's largest living organism, a grove of connected aspen trees. In fall, the aspens turn golden and orange, creating a peaceful and colorful setting for hikes near Fish Lake.

Winter: Winter Wonderlands

Winter turns Utah into a snowy paradise, offering a variety of activities for visitors who love cold weather. From skiing on world-class slopes to exploring snow-covered red rock landscapes, Utah is a winter wonderland.

- **Park City and Deer Valley**: These famous ski resorts offer excellent slopes, cozy lodges, and festive winter events. Whether you enjoy skiing, snowboarding, or relaxing après-ski activities, these resorts are perfect for winter fun.

- **Arches National Park**: Visiting Arches in winter is a quieter experience, as the crowds are smaller. The red sandstone formations, like Delicate Arch, look even more stunning when dusted with snow. Trails are less crowded, and the scenery is ideal for winter photography.

- **Bryce Canyon National Park**: Bryce's hoodoos look magical under a layer of snow. Activities like snowshoeing and cross-country skiing are popular, and the clear winter skies make it a great place for stargazing even in the colder months.

Each season in Utah offers its own unique charm and activities. Whether you're hiking among spring wildflowers, gazing at the stars in summer, admiring fall foliage, or enjoying winter adventures, Utah is a place where every season brings something extraordinary to discover.

HIDDEN GEMS AND SCENIC DRIVES

Utah is famous for its well-known national parks, but it also has many hidden gems and scenic drives that are just as amazing. These quieter spots let you explore unique landscapes, see wildlife, and enjoy Utah's natural beauty at a slower pace.

Goblin Valley State Park: Otherworldly Formations

Goblin Valley State Park is a truly unique place, filled with rock formations that look like mushrooms, goblins, and other strange shapes. These sandstone structures were formed over millions of years by erosion and weathering, creating a landscape that feels like another planet.

- **Hiking and Exploring**: The park has short, easy trails that take you right into the "goblins." Both kids and adults love walking through the formations and discovering the unusual shapes up close.

- **Goblin's Lair**: One of the park's highlights is Goblin's Lair, a hidden chamber within the rocks. Getting there requires a short hike with some scrambling, adding a sense of adventure to your visit.

- **Photography**: The reddish-orange colors of the sandstone make this park a favorite for photographers, especially during sunrise or sunset, when the light creates dramatic shadows on the formations.

Dead Horse Point State Park: Dramatic Overlooks

Dead Horse Point State Park is well-known for its incredible views of the Colorado River and the canyonlands surrounding it. While its name comes from a local legend, the park itself is stunning and full of beauty.

- **Dead Horse Point Overlook:** The main overlook gives visitors a breathtaking view of the Colorado River winding through the canyon, almost 2,000 feet below. The layers of rock and vast views make it a perfect spot for reflection and photography.

- **Hiking Trails**: The park has several trails, like the East Rim Trail and West Rim Trail, which are easy to moderate in difficulty. These trails follow the canyon's edge, providing spectacular views along the way.

- **Biking**: Mountain bikers will enjoy the Intrepid Trail System, which has thrilling routes for all skill levels. The trails offer fun challenges and incredible scenery.

- **Stargazing**: Thanks to the park's remote location and minimal light pollution, it's a fantastic spot for stargazing. The clear skies offer amazing views of stars, constellations, and even the Milky Way.

Antelope Island: Wildlife and Serenity

Antelope Island, located in the Great Salt Lake, is a peaceful escape where you can enjoy stunning scenery and observe wildlife in its natural habitat.

It's a great destination for those who want to avoid crowds and relax in nature.

- **Wildlife Watching:** The island is home to a large population of bison that roam freely. Visitors can also see pronghorn antelope, mule deer, coyotes, and various bird species, such as pelicans and hawks.

- **Scenic Trails**: Antelope Island has several hiking trails, like the Buffalo Point Trail and Frary Peak Trail. These trails offer incredible views of the lake and mountains, with Frary Peak providing the best vistas from the highest point on the island.

- **Great Salt Lake Beaches**: The island's beaches are a great place to relax. You can float effortlessly in the saltwater or enjoy a peaceful picnic while taking in the scenery.

- **Sunsets and Photography**: Antelope Island is famous for its stunning sunsets. The vibrant colors reflect off the Great Salt Lake, creating dramatic and serene scenes that photographers love to capture.

These hidden gems and scenic drives give visitors a quieter way to experience Utah's incredible beauty.

Whether you're wandering through Goblin Valley's strange formations, soaking in the views at Dead Horse Point, or enjoying the peace and wildlife of Antelope Island, these spots highlight Utah's amazing diversity and charm.

Coral Pink Sand Dunes State Park

Coral Pink Sand Dunes State Park is a hidden gem in southern Utah, known for its striking dunes of soft, pink-colored sand. Formed over thousands of years by wind erosion from the nearby Navajo sandstone cliffs, the park offers a unique and tranquil desert experience.

- **Sandboarding and Sledding**: The dunes are perfect for adventurous activities like sandboarding and sledding. Visitors can rent equipment from nearby shops and glide down the smooth slopes for an exhilarating experience.

- **Hiking**: The park features several trails that allow you to explore the dunes and surrounding desert. The Nature Trail is an easy option, providing insights into the park's geology and wildlife.

- **Photography**: The vibrant pink sand set against the blue sky and surrounding red rock cliffs creates a stunning landscape for photographers. Sunrise and sunset are particularly magical times to capture the beauty of the dunes.

- **Off-Roading**: A portion of the dunes is open to off-highway vehicles (OHVs), offering a thrilling way to explore the area. Riders can enjoy the challenge of navigating the shifting sands while taking in the breathtaking scenery.

This peaceful and less-crowded park is a must-visit for those looking to experience Utah's diverse landscapes.

Highway 12: America's Most Beautiful Drive

Highway 12, often called "America's Most Beautiful Drive," is a scenic byway that winds through some of Utah's most breathtaking landscapes. Stretching for 122 miles between Bryce Canyon National Park and Capitol Reef National Park, this drive is an unforgettable journey through red rock canyons, alpine forests, and high desert vistas.

- **Red Canyon**: As you begin the drive near Bryce Canyon, you'll pass through Red Canyon, with its vibrant red cliffs and towering rock formations. The Pink Ledges Trail offers a short hike to enjoy the scenery up close.

- **Grand Staircase-Escalante National Monument:** This section of the byway features dramatic cliffs, deep canyons, and rugged terrain. Stops like Calf Creek Falls provide opportunities for scenic hikes, with the lower falls being a popular destination for its picturesque waterfall and lush surroundings.

- **Boulder Mountain**: The byway climbs to over 9,000 feet as it crosses Boulder Mountain, offering panoramic views of the surrounding valleys and distant plateaus. During fall, the aspen forests along this stretch turn brilliant shades of gold.

- **Hogback Ridge:** This narrow stretch of the road is one of the most famous parts of Highway 12. The ridge has steep drop-offs on both sides, providing heart-pounding views of the canyons below.

Highway 12 is a journey as much as a destination, with countless opportunities to stop and explore the stunning landscapes along the way.

Scenic Byway 24: Through Capitol Reef National Park

Scenic Byway 24 cuts through the heart of Capitol Reef National Park, offering a stunning drive that showcases the park's unique geological formations and striking desert landscapes. Stretching from Loa to Hanksville, this route is a perfect way to experience the beauty of Capitol Reef from the comfort of your car.

- **Fruita Historic District**: This lush oasis along the Fremont River is a highlight of the drive. Visitors can see historic structures, orchards, and remnants of the pioneer settlement that once thrived here. During harvest season, you can even pick fresh fruit from the orchards.

- **Capitol Dome and Waterpocket Fold:** The drive provides fantastic views of Capitol Dome, a white sandstone formation that resembles the U.S. Capitol building, and the Waterpocket Fold, a massive geologic monocline that stretches for nearly 100 miles.

- **Hickman Bridge Trail**: A short hike from the byway leads to Hickman Bridge, a natural sandstone arch that is one of the park's most popular features. The trail offers stunning views of the surrounding cliffs and river.

- **Chimney Rock and Goosenecks Overlook:** These roadside stops provide dramatic views of Capitol Reef's layered rock formations and the winding Fremont River below.

Scenic Byway 24 is more than just a road, it's a gateway to the wonders of Capitol Reef, offering both convenience and beauty for those exploring this lesser-visited national park.

CULTURAL AND HISTORICAL ATTRACTIONS

Utah's history and culture are closely tied to its remarkable landscapes and the communities that have shaped its identity over time. From sacred religious sites to prehistoric fossils and ancient ruins, Utah offers visitors the chance to immerse themselves in a fascinating journey through its past. Below is a detailed exploration of some of Utah's most significant cultural and historical attractions.

Salt Lake City: The Mormon Tabernacle and Temple Square

Salt Lake City serves as Utah's cultural and spiritual hub, with Temple Square standing as its most iconic landmark. Spanning 10 acres, this historic complex is the global headquarters of the Church of Jesus Christ of Latter-day Saints (LDS) and draws millions of visitors each year.

•**Salt Lake Temple**: Built over 40 years and completed in 1893, the Salt Lake Temple is a masterpiece of Gothic-inspired architecture. With six spires and sturdy granite walls, it is one of Utah's most recognizable buildings. Although the temple's interior is only open to church members, the exterior and surrounding grounds are accessible to all visitors, who can learn about its history at the Visitors' Centers.

•**The Tabernacle**: Constructed in 1867, the Tabernacle is famous for its unique dome-shaped roof, which was built without nails. The building's exceptional acoustics make it a world-class concert venue, and guests can enjoy free weekly performances by the renowned Tabernacle Choir at Temple Square and organ recitals.

•**Church History Museum**: This museum offers an engaging look at the history of the Mormon pioneers, featuring rare artifacts, interactive displays, and artwork that tell the story of their migration to Utah and the development of their community.

•**Gardens and Seasonal Events**: The beautifully landscaped gardens of Temple Square change throughout the year, offering a peaceful place to stroll. During the holiday season, the square becomes a dazzling display of lights and nativity scenes, creating a magical atmosphere.

Temple Square is much more than a religious center, it is also a place of learning, culture, and reflection, welcoming people of all backgrounds to explore its history and beauty.

Dinosaur National Monument: Fossils and Prehistoric Wonders

Located on the border of Utah and Colorado, Dinosaur National Monument is a world-renowned site for its incredible collection of dinosaur fossils and striking landscapes. It's a perfect destination for those interested in both natural history and outdoor adventure.

•**Quarry Exhibit Hall**: This exhibit is the centerpiece of the monument, showcasing over 1,500 dinosaur fossils embedded in a rock wall. Visitors can see bones from species such as Allosaurus and Stegosaurus, and some fossils are even available for touching. The interactive exhibits provide insights into the lives of these ancient creatures and how they were preserved in the rock.

•**Fossil Discovery Trail**: This short trail begins at the quarry and passes several fossil beds where visitors can see remnants of dinosaurs in their natural setting. Interpretive signs along the trail explain the geology and history of the area.

•**Petroglyphs and Pictographs**: The monument is also rich in cultural history, with numerous rock art panels left behind by the Fremont people. These petroglyphs depict animals, humans, and symbolic designs that offer a glimpse into life thousands of years ago. Sites like Swelter Shelter and Cub Creek feature some of the best examples.

•**Outdoor Adventures**: Beyond its historical significance, the monument's canyons and rivers provide opportunities for rafting, kayaking, and hiking. Trails like Harpers Corner and Jones Hole offer stunning views of the rugged landscape.

Dinosaur National Monument is a destination that combines education with adventure, offering a unique way to explore Utah's prehistoric past and natural beauty.

Ancestral Puebloan Sites in Bears Ears National Monument

Bears Ears National Monument in southeastern Utah is a sacred and historically significant area, home to thousands of archaeological sites that date back over a thousand years. This monument is an important cultural and spiritual space for many Native American tribes.

•**Cedar Mesa and Cliff Dwellings**: Cedar Mesa is one of the most significant areas in Bears Ears, featuring well-preserved cliff dwellings like House on Fire and Moon House. These structures, built into the cliffs by the Ancestral Puebloans, showcase their ingenuity and ability to adapt to the harsh desert environment.

•**Rock Art Panels**: The monument is famous for its ancient rock art, including petroglyphs and pictographs left by the Fremont and Ancestral Puebloan peoples. Newspaper Rock is one of the most notable sites, featuring hundreds of intricate carvings that tell stories and depict daily life.

•**Spiritual Importance:** Bears Ears is considered sacred by the Navajo, Hopi, Ute, Zuni, and other Native American tribes. For these communities, the land holds deep spiritual meaning and serves as a connection to their ancestors. Visitors can take tribal-led tours to learn about the area's cultural and spiritual significance directly from Native guides.

•**Hiking and Exploration**: Bears Ears offers miles of trails that lead to hidden ruins, scenic overlooks, and rock art sites. Trails like Butler Wash and Arch Canyon are popular for their mix of natural beauty and historical treasures.

Bears Ears National Monument is a unique destination where visitors can connect with the ancient history, culture, and spirituality of the region.

Conclusion

These cultural and historical attractions offer a deeper understanding of Utah's past, from the faith-driven legacy of Salt Lake City to the prehistoric wonders of Dinosaur National Monument and the ancient sites of Bears Ears. Each location tells a unique story and invites visitors to explore and appreciate the state's rich heritage.

ECO-TOURISM AND RESPONSIBLE TRAVEL

Utah's stunning landscapes, from vibrant red rock canyons to lush alpine forests, draw millions of visitors every year. With such incredible beauty comes the responsibility to protect and preserve these environments for future generations. Eco-tourism in Utah encourages visitors to minimize their environmental impact, practice sustainable habits, and support local communities. Here's how you can enjoy Utah's natural wonders while being a responsible traveler.

Preserving Utah's Natural Beauty

Utah's diverse ecosystems, including delicate deserts, crystal-clear rivers, and dense forests, need care and respect to stay pristine.

- **Stay on Designated Trails:** Always stick to marked paths while hiking or biking. Going off-trail can harm fragile ecosystems like cryptobiotic soil in desert areas. Staying on the trail protects plants and wildlife.

- **Respect Wildlife:** Observe animals from a safe distance and never feed them. Feeding wildlife can harm their health and disrupt their natural behavior.

- **Avoid Taking Natural Items:** Leave rocks, plants, and other natural objects where they are. These elements are essential to the environment and should remain undisturbed for everyone to enjoy.

- **Reduce Plastic Waste**: Bring a reusable water bottle and avoid single-use plastics. Many parks provide refill stations to help reduce waste.

Leave No Trace Principles

The Leave No Trace guidelines help visitors minimize their impact on the environment while enjoying outdoor adventures.

1. Plan Ahead and Prepare: Check the rules and regulations for your destination and pack accordingly. Be ready for sudden changes in weather, especially in remote areas.

2. Travel and Camp on Durable Surfaces: Stick to established campsites and trails to prevent erosion and damage to the landscape.

3. Dispose of Waste Properly: Take all your trash, leftover food, and hygiene items with you. If there are no restrooms, learn the proper methods for waste disposal.

4. Leave What You Find: Avoid picking flowers, disturbing ancient sites, or collecting souvenirs like rocks and fossils.

5. Minimize Campfire Impact: Use a camp stove when possible. If campfires are allowed, keep them small and only use designated fire rings. Fully extinguish fires before leaving.

6. Respect Wildlife: Watch animals from a distance and avoid disturbing them. Stay quiet to avoid causing stress or danger.

7. Be Considerate of Others: Keep noise to a minimum, yield to others on trails, and respect the privacy of fellow visitors.

By following these principles, you can help protect Utah's natural beauty for future generations.

Supporting Local Communities

Eco-tourism isn't just about protecting nature, it's also about helping the people who live in the areas you visit.

•**Shop Local:** Support small businesses by buying handmade goods, crafts, and souvenirs. Local farmers' markets and artisan shops offer unique items while boosting the community's economy.

•**Stay in Locally Owned Lodging**: Choose family-run hotels, bed-and-breakfasts, or campgrounds to directly support Utah's residents.

•**Dine at Local Restaurants**: Eat at locally owned establishments instead of chain restaurants. This helps local chefs and gives you a chance to try authentic Utah flavors.

•**Hire Local Guides:** Join guided tours led by local experts for activities like hiking, rafting, or exploring. Not only does this enhance your experience, but it also supports local livelihoods.

•**Volunteer Opportunities:** Participate in cleanup events or trail maintenance through groups like the Utah Conservation Corps or park organizations.

This is a great way to give back to the areas you visit.

In Conclusion

By practicing eco-tourism and traveling responsibly, you can help protect Utah's natural beauty, support its local communities, and ensure that future visitors can enjoy the same incredible experiences. Together, we can preserve what makes Utah so special.

PRACTICAL TRAVEL TIPS

Planning a trip to Utah takes some preparation to make sure you have the best time possible. Whether it's choosing the perfect season, packing the right gear, or navigating the state's scenic routes, these tips will help you enjoy a smooth and memorable adventure.

When to Visit Utah for the Best Experience

Each season in Utah offers unique activities and attractions, so the best time to visit depends on what you want to do.

Spring (March to May):

Spring is ideal for hiking and exploring national parks like Zion, Arches, and Bryce Canyon. Temperatures are mild, and wildflowers are in bloom. This is also a quieter time before summer crowds arrive.

Weather: Daytime temperatures range from 60°F to 80°F, with cooler mornings and evenings.

Summer (June to August):

Summer is perfect for higher-elevation destinations like Park City and the Wasatch Mountains, where it's cooler. It's also a great time for water activities at Lake Powell and Bear Lake.

Weather: Southern Utah can be extremely hot, with temperatures over 100°F. Plan outdoor activities early in the morning or late in the evening.

Fall (September to November):

Fall is popular for its cooler weather and stunning fall foliage. The Alpine Loop Scenic Byway and Fishlake National Forest are must-see spots for vibrant autumn colors.

Weather: Comfortable daytime temperatures between 50°F and 70°F, with crisp, cool nights.

Winter (December to February):

Winter turns Utah into a snowy paradise, ideal for skiing and snowboarding at resorts like Park City, Deer Valley, and Snowbird. National parks such as Arches and Bryce Canyon are quieter and look beautiful under snow.

Weather: Heavy snowfall in mountain areas, while southern Utah remains milder with temperatures between 30°F and 50°F.

Packing Essentials for Every Season

Packing the right gear is key to staying comfortable and prepared for Utah's changing weather and activities.

Spring and Fall:

- **Clothing**: Layered outfits to stay warm in the mornings and evenings while being comfortable during warmer days.

- **Gear**: Comfortable hiking boots, a daypack, and sunscreen.

- **Hydration**: Bring a reusable water bottle for hikes and outdoor adventures.

Summer:

- **Clothing**: Lightweight, breathable clothing with hats and sunglasses for sun protection.

- **Water Gear**: Swimsuits, water shoes, and towels for Lake Powell or Bear Lake activities.

- **Bug Protection**: Bug spray is a must, especially near water.

Winter:

- **Clothing**: Insulated jackets, gloves, hats, and thermal layers for snow activities.

- **Snow Gear**: Waterproof boots, ski pants, and goggles for skiing or hiking in snowy conditions.

- **Driving Safety**: Chains or snow tires if driving in mountainous areas.

Year-Round Essentials:

- **Electronics**: A camera or smartphone to capture Utah's stunning scenery.

- **Navigation**: Maps or a GPS device, as cell service can be spotty in remote areas.

- **Safety**: A first-aid kit for minor injuries.

Road Trip Tips and Navigating Utah's Scenic Routes

Utah's scenic byways and dramatic landscapes make road trips one of the best ways to explore the state.

Plan Your Route:

- Research top scenic drives like Highway 12, Scenic Byway 24, and the Alpine Loop. Include rest stops and gas stations in your plan, especially in remote areas.

- Must-visit destinations include the "Mighty Five" national parks: Zion, Bryce Canyon, Arches, Canyonlands, and Capitol Reef.

Prepare Your Vehicle:

- Before starting your trip, check your car's tires, brakes, and fluids. If you're renting, consider a 4WD or high-clearance vehicle for rougher terrain.

- Carry a spare tire, jumper cables, and an emergency kit for unexpected situations.

Pack for the Drive:

- Bring snacks, water, and a cooler to store perishables.

- Load entertainment options like music, audiobooks, or podcasts for long stretches of driving.

Drive Safely:

- Stick to speed limits and watch for wildlife, especially during early morning or evening hours.

- Avoid driving at night in rural areas, as roads can be dark, and wildlife may cross.

- Keep an eye on weather conditions, as rain or snow can make some roads dangerous or inaccessible.

Explore Responsibly:

- Take your time to enjoy Utah's views and stop at designated pullouts for photos.

- Follow the "leave no trace" principle by taking all your trash with you and disposing of it properly.

Utah's natural beauty, combined with its well-maintained roads and parks, makes it an incredible destination for all types of travelers. By choosing the right time to visit, packing smartly, and following these road trip tips, you'll create unforgettable memories while enjoying everything Utah has to offer.

LOCATION, ADDRESS
AND COORDINATES

Here is the list of accommodations Unique dining and top Attractions mentioned in these guide, along with their addresses and approximate coordinates:

ACCOMMODATION

1. Grand America Hotel

Address: 555 S Main St, Salt Lake City, UT 84111

Coordinates: 40.7587° N, 111.8911° W

2. Amangiri

Address: 1 Kayenta Road, Canyon Point, UT 84741

Coordinates: 37.0161° N, 111.6208° W

3. Stein Eriksen Lodge Deer Valley

Address: 7700 Stein Way, Park City, UT 84060

Coordinates: 40.6222° N, 111.4906° W

4. Cliffrose Springdale

Address: 281 Zion Park Blvd, Springdale, UT 84767

Coordinates: 37.1909° N, 112.9944° W

5. Sorrel River Ranch Resort & Spa

Address: Mile 17, Highway 128, Moab, UT 84532

Coordinates: 38.6384° N, 109.4524° W

6. The St. Regis Deer Valley

Address: 2300 Deer Valley Drive East, Park City, UT 84060

Coordinates: 40.6376° N, 111.4781° W

7. Zermatt Utah Resort & Spa

Address: 784 W Resort Dr, Midway, UT 84049

Coordinates: 40.5148° N, 111.4749° W

8. Desert Pearl Inn

Address: 707 Zion Park Blvd, Springdale, UT 84767

Coordinates: 37.1935° N, 112.9961° W

9. The Lodge at Bryce Canyon

Address: Bryce Canyon National Park, UT 84764

Coordinates: 37.6278° N, 112.1677° W

RESTAURANTS AND UNIQUE DINING

1. Red Iguana

Address: 736 W North Temple, Salt Lake City, UT 84116

Coordinates: 40.7726° N, 111.9102° W

Description: A beloved Mexican restaurant known for its authentic mole sauces and vibrant atmosphere.

2. Red Iguana 2

Address: 866 W South Temple, Salt Lake City, UT 84104

Coordinates: 40.7723° N, 111.9168° W

Description: The second location of the famous Red Iguana, offering the same authentic Mexican cuisine with more seating.

3. Eva's Bakery

Address: 155 S Main St, Salt Lake City, UT 84111

Coordinates: 40.7675° N, 111.8910° W

Description: A French-inspired bakery and café featuring artisan bread, pastries, and delightful breakfast and lunch options.

4. Grub Steak Restaurant

Address: 2200 Sidewinder Dr, Park City, UT 84060

Coordinates: 40.6618° N, 111.4975° W

Description: A steakhouse offering hearty steaks, fresh seafood, and a cozy Western atmosphere.

5. Riverhorse on Main

Address: 540 Main St, Park City, UT 84060

Coordinates: 40.6462° N, 111.4980° W

Description: An upscale restaurant known for creative dishes like macadamia nut-crusted halibut and wild game meatloaf.

6. Hell's Backbone Grill & Farm

Address: 20 N Highway 12, Boulder, UT 84716

Coordinates: 37.9061° N, 111.4233° W

Description: An award-winning farm-to-table restaurant focusing on sustainable dishes using locally sourced ingredients.

7. Oscar's Café

Address: 948 Zion Park Blvd, Springdale, UT 84767

Coordinates: 37.1887° N, 112.9980° W

Description: A casual spot offering generous portions and Southwestern-inspired dishes near Zion National Park.

8. Capitol Reef Inn & Café

Address: 825 UT-24, Torrey, UT 84775

Coordinates: 38.3006° N, 111.4209° W

Description: A cozy café with home-style cooking, serving hearty breakfasts and traditional pies near Capitol Reef National Park.

9. Slackwater Pub & Pizzeria

Address: 1895 Washington Blvd, Ogden, UT 84401

Coordinates: 41.2423° N, 111.9727° W

Description: A creative pizzeria with a wide selection of craft beers, popular for its unique toppings like smoked trout.

TOP ATTRACTIONS

National Parks

1. Zion National Park

Address: 1 Zion Park Blvd, Springdale, UT 84767

Coordinates: 37.2982° N, 113.0263° W

2. Bryce Canyon National Park

Address: Hwy 63, Bryce Canyon, UT 84764

Coordinates: 37.5930° N, 112.1871° W

3. Arches National Park

Address: Main Park Rd, Moab, UT 84532

Coordinates: 38.7331° N, 109.5925° W

4. Canyonlands National Park

Address: 2282 SW Resource Blvd, Moab, UT 84532

Coordinates: 38.3269° N, 109.8783° W

5. Capitol Reef National Park

Address: HC 70 Box 15, Torrey, UT 84775

Coordinates: 38.3670° N, 111.2615° W

State Parks and Scenic Spots

6. Dead Horse Point State Park

Address: UT-313, Moab, UT 84532

Coordinates: 38.4698° N, 109.7425° W

7. Goblin Valley State Park

Address: Goblin Valley Rd, Green River, UT 84525

Coordinates: 38.5720° N, 110.7074° W

8. Antelope Island State Park

Address: 4528 W 1700 S, Syracuse, UT 84075

Coordinates: 40.9570° N, 112.1975° W

9. Coral Pink Sand Dunes State Park

Address: 12500 Sand Dune Rd, Kanab, UT 84741

Coordinates: 37.0583° N, 112.6646° W

Cultural and Historical Attractions

10. Temple Square

Address: 50 N Temple, Salt Lake City, UT 84150

Coordinates: 40.7706° N, 111.8910° W

11. Dinosaur National Monument

Address: 11625 E 1500 S, Jensen, UT 84035

Coordinates: 40.4406° N, 109.3046° W

12. Bears Ears National Monument

Address: Highway 95, Blanding, UT 84511

Coordinates: 37.5683° N, 109.8281° W

13. Monument Valley Navajo Tribal Park

Address: US-163, Oljato-Monument Valley, UT 84536

Coordinates: 36.9986° N, 110.0984° W

Popular Cities and Resorts

14. Park City Mountain Resort

Address: 1345 Lowell Ave, Park City, UT 84060

Coordinates: 40.6514° N, 111.5079° W

15. Salt Lake City (General)

Coordinates: 40.7608° N, 111.8910° W

MAPS

Google Map QR Code

Made in United States
Troutdale, OR
03/28/2025